Transform Your Life with One Call

Volume 1

America's Top Life Coaches Reveal What You Need to Know

SociaVerse Publishing

DEDICATION

For Dad, the ultimate Life Coach.

TABLE OF CONTENTS

PREFACE

By all indications, it was a normal morning. I was delivering newspapers in a neighborhood about a mile away from my mother's house. A man walking the street flagged me down, telling me that he didn't get his newspaper because I missed his house. The next words out of his mouth rocked me to my core.

"Get out of the car, or I'll shoot you!"

"What?" I asked, fearfully.

"Get out of the car or I'll shoot your a**!" he threatened, as he opened my door and grabbed my wrist.

I complied hastily, hopping out of my car. In a moment of clarity, I put the car in Neutral instead of Park so the car rolled down the street. He was forced to let go of my wrist to chase the car down. He hopped in while I stood and watched him drive away.

Why was I in this situation? What was I doing delivering newspapers at 25 years old that I would even be in a position to be carjacked?

In early 2001, my first son was months into his new life. We were in Philadelphia. I was in the mortgage business, and every day at work crushed my soul. I left my job, virtually penniless, save for the unemployment checks. We moved back home to the Washington, DC area. Home, to my mother's basement. A low moment in my life, to be sure, relegated to charity at a time when my career should have started flourishing.

Here, I had breakthrough moment number one: my beautiful and supportive wife, knowing that I had a talent for computer work, signed me up for IT certification classes without my knowledge. I had always been resistant to pursue an IT career because I couldn't understand why someone would pay me for something that came so easily to me. Regardless, I went along with it, took some aptitude tests, and, sure enough, it was a career I had to pursue. I was done with the mortgage business for good.

Still, without a job, we needed cash flow. The only employment I could find was delivering newspapers for *The Washington Post*. I had no formal experience in Information Technology, so the delivery job would have to sustain us until I could break into the industry. That meant I would need to get up at 3 AM every single morning, including weekends and holidays, to deliver 'papes' for two hours. And so it was, on one fateful morning during my three year tenure as a paperboy, that my life was threatened.

The details of that morning could fill another volume. Suffice it to say that I was unscathed, that I got my car back, and that the perpetrator ended up in jail. And I finished my deliveries for that morning.

In the meantime, I had breakthrough moment number two: my wife's aunt, Anne Conlan, offered to 'work with me'. At the time, I didn't know what that meant, or what it entailed, but I needed all the help I could get. As it turned out, Aunt Anne is a Life Coach.

I went over to her house regularly. We talked; she asked questions; we talked some more. She saw something in me that I couldn't see. I was too mired in my own problems to realize what I had to offer the world. She helped me see it. Then she helped me reach breakthrough moment number three: my first IT job.

It was an entry-level job. The pay was not much more than what I had been making in the mortgage business. But it was the foot in the door that I so desperately needed — the starting point of my new career in a field that accommodated my natural talents.

Since then, my life's trajectory has trended sharply upwards. My career in IT grew rapidly, and I have been paid handsomely for my work. All things considered, all was well. But I wanted more. It had always been a lifelong dream of mine to be in business for myself. What better way, then, to combine a natural talent with long-desired aspirations than to help businesses market themselves on the Internet? I had dabbled with the idea in 1996 while still in college. I learned more about it during the newspaper delivery era. In 2005, I opened shop with my first client. From there, business grew astronomically, as I was able to generate millions of dollars in revenue for my clients.

My personal success grew as well, allowing me to pursue my love of traveling and visiting places all around the world. I've been skydiving in Fiji, paragliding in Switzerland, whitewater sledging in New Zealand, dog sledding in Alaska, and snorkeling in the Great Barrier Reef, to name but a few.

My children's lives have also been enriched as a result. Instead of reading about art, they've been to the Louvre. Instead of watching "Annie" on television, they visited an orphanage in Fiji. Instead of watching a World War II documentary, they visited a concentration camp in Dachau, Germany.

Indeed, my family and I have lived a life that is full of life. I am incredibly fortunate, and for that I am incredibly grateful. It all started with a Life Coach.

This book is written and compiled from that place of gratitude. I have made it my personal mission to make as many Life Coaches as I can become as successful as I can help them to be. It is my way of giving back to the noblest of all professions, and to the wonderful and deserving people who comprise it. I write this book for you, dear coaches, to showcase who you are, what you can do, and why working with you is the best decision for a person to make.

At the same time, I have also made it my mission to help every individual who needs a coach to be able to benefit from one. You, dear reader, may be at a point in your life that resembles where I was in mine during my newspaper delivery era. You are at rock bottom, whether it be in your career, in your relationships, in your health, in your faith, in your finances, or in your life in general. All you need is the right person to come along and help set your guidance systems along the right path, like Aunt Anne did for me. I write this book for you, that you may understand your choices and dispel any misconceptions you harbor about coaching, and that you find your Aunt Anne.

If I am successful in my mission, even for just one coach and just one protégé, lives are changed for the positive. Those changed lives radiate outwardly a ripple effect for all those connected to them. One by one, as lives change, so, too, will the world, and all of us are better for it.

ACKNOWLEDGMENTS

I'd like to thank the top Life Coaches in America whose contributions of time and effort made this book possible:

Judith Auslander of Wise Heart Coaching & Hypnosis;

Angela Ambrosia of LoveandRelationshipCoach.com;

Kerry Labendz of Kerry Labendz – Life Coach;

Grant M. Ingle, PhD of Grant M. Ingle and Associates;

Kellee Tyler of A Goal Achieved, LLC.;

Jalaal Aleem Madyun of JAM Life Coaching;

Iris Fanning of Iris Fanning Coaching;

Clary Torres of Clary Torres Intl.;

Nina Elisa Segura of Metaspire;

Colette D. Ellis of InStep Consulting LLC;

Thank you to the hardworking staff of SociaVerse Publishing, who are the engine that moves us forward.

My eternal gratitude to Anne Conlan, the coach who launched my star.

And to my beautiful wife Bernadette and incredible children Nico, Julianna, and Samantha. This has always been, will always be, for you.

INTRODUCTION

When we watch the artistry of our favorite athletes, musicians, singers, and actors, we watch the ease with which they execute their craft. The flawlessness of their technique; the absolute mastery and majesty of their world.

Undoubtedly, hour upon tireless hour went into the making of the final product. And yet behind every hour is a coach who guided the direction of that hour. After all, what good is practice if spent practicing imperfection?

People don't view their own lives through the lens of artistry or mastery. Indeed, most people literally stumble and fumble their way from day to day. Imperfect practice in practice.

Why does it have to be that way? Why not have a family life executed with ease? Why not run a business or career performed with flawless technique? Why not master what life has to offer, experience fulfillment, and really become open to the majesty of what your world can become?

It is all there for the taking. All it takes is the proper guidance for the hour upon tireless hour spent in the endeavor. All it takes is the help of a coach.

In these pages we interviewed some of the top coaches in America, each of whom have their own specialty, area of expertise, and the ability to guide those who seek their assistance down the path of a fulfilling existence. Learn about them. Engage them. And let them take you to where you know you deserve to be.

CHAPTER 1

Judith Auslander

What is a Life Coach, and what do you do?

As a Life Coach our coaching sessions focus on the present and on what the client can do to create the future they want. A weekly 50 minute session can be either in person or over the phone.

Generally, coaching consists of:

- Finding ease through transitions

- Rearranging the jumbled jigsaw puzzle of the client's life back into a beautiful picture

- Achieving their goals

- Clarifying their values to discover their passion, purpose and mission in life

Coaching is different from traditional talk therapy in that we don't focus on the past, but rather on the desired future. I pay close attention to what the client is saying in order to make sure that he/she is speaking in the positive and avoiding self-limiting language.

I do this by asking provocative questions, to help stimulate new ideas, concepts and creativity. In return, I offer open, honest, and necessary feedback that will speed their journey to the life they deeply desire. I help inspire them with new ideas, concepts, strategies and frameworks that help reorient around success as they define it.

Why would someone need a Life Coach?

Usually it is when they feel stuck — that life is just not moving forward as they hoped or wished it would. Often the client finds himself or herself responding to the same stimulus in the same negative way.

Traditional talk therapy is great for many different issues, but for getting unstuck, life coaching is quick and a lot more cost effective.

In my particular coaching practice, I work with individuals looking to change something in their life that isn't working, setting and achieving goals, and resolving relationship issues. I also work with small business owners who are starting out.

How do I select a Life Coach?

First I feel it is important that you select a coach who is trained through an accredited ICF (International Coaching Federation) school. Unfortunately, there are not any legal credentials to hang a shingle declaring oneself a coach. To be sure to find a coach who is trained through an accredited school, you can ask them what school they went to.

You also want to make sure that your coach continues their training through being a part of their local ICF group, continues to take classes, and has references on their website of past clients.

Now, even more important than this, you want to interview your coach and find out if they are someone you resonate with. Coaching is a very personal conversation and you want to make sure that you feel totally relaxed with your coach.

How does coaching work?

Coaches have their own program or plan. I have my 12 week program to a new life. Prior to the first session I send out a lot of paperwork to fill out. This paperwork helps me to get to know the client and their needs. So the first session is generally about 90 minutes long and is spent going over the paperwork, getting to know the client, and really defining his/her goals for our 12 weeks together.

The second and third sessions are spent getting to know how best to coach the client, what his/her personally needs are to succeed. As we move along, the coaching sessions begin to become more intensive.

Around the fourth session I send out the CVI (Core Value Index Assessment), which will really hone in on his/her core values and why the client reacts to certain situations the way they do.

Each of our sessions will include work for the client to do at home to help incorporate the skills they will be learning.

By week six shifts are happening and I do a check in to see how things are going, to make sure the client's goals are on target.

By Week twelve their life has made some gigantic changes. The client notes how behaviors have changed and modified. They will be on their way toward the life they want.

How much does Life Coaching typically cost?

Each coach is different. Usually coaching is around $100 - $200 per session. I have a special for my 12 week program.

What happens during a coaching session?

Generally there is a check in of how things have gone since the last session. What are the clients wins and what helped them to achieve those wins? Where have they felt less success — what are their challenges? These challenges are usually what we focus on during the session.

What are your areas of specialty?

My particular areas of specialty are women between the ages of 40 to 75. These are generally women who desire change — to get 'unstuck'. These are women who have run a company or a household, but now realize that they want something more.

These are often women who have:

- Worked while hiding their deepest desires
- Gone through life doing what they 'need' to do while neglecting their heart's longings for something different
- Tended to say "yes," when they really want to say "no"

- Covered up their feelings and emotions

- Tended to give more than they received

- Ignored their spiritual coreWhat I have noticed is that most women's stories have the same theme: I am unhappy; I am unfilled; I am unsure where to go next. I also work with couples and female solopreneurs who are starting out. I also very much enjoy teaching group classes in goal setting and working on how we sabotage ourselves. Most of all, I bring a spiritual element to my coaching. I call myself a Wisdom Guide.

What do you go over in the first session?

The first session is a very special one and usually lasts about 90 minutes. During this session we go over all the paperwork I sent out prior to our first meeting. I want to know what has been going on in the client's life—what have been their successes, what brings them joy. Of course, I also want to discover where the pain is. Most importantly, I want to know their goals and how much they are willing to work toward them.

I have them take a values test to see where their goals are in alignment to their values. This is very important.

I also want to know who will support them and be part of their team during their change.

How long are the coaching sessions, and how often should I go?

Coaching sessions are generally weekly and about 1 hour

long.

What are the benefits of having a Life Coach?

Have a life coach is kind of like having a fairy godmother. Most of us try to do everything alone. That's OK, unless it is not working. A coach can become the person who really looks at what the client has been doing and helps them to see where changes may need to be made and how to make those changes.

The most important thing about a Life Coach is that they don't give you the answers. Rather, they help you to find the answers that work for you that come from you. Much more empowering.

How can I tell if a Life Coach is any good?

You don't want a Life Coach who tells you what to do. Coaches don't tell you what to do; they guide you toward creating your own decisions. A good Life Coach should ask a lot of questions and be more of a listener than a talker.

How long must I commit to working with a coach?

I would give it at least 3 months.

Can I hire a Life Coach for a short-term, special project?

Yes, a coach can be great for just helping with a one-time project that just needs that extra push — someone to bounce ideas off of.

Why would people who are already successful hire a Life

Coach?

Because trying to do everything alone is too limiting. A successful entrepreneur, businessperson, CEO, homemaker—whomever—needs to hear more than their own thoughts. Also, a Life Coach helps you to think outside of your own bubble.

Do you offer coaching remotely, either online or over the phone, or do you only see local clients?

I have coached in person, over the phone, over SKYPE—nearly any medium will do.

Please tell us how readers can get in contact with you here:

Judith Auslander, MA, CLC, CHt

http://www.WiseHeartCoaching.com

Judith@WiseHeartCoaching.com

503-318-9343

I am a Life Coach, Hypnotherapist, Reiki & EFT Practitioner.

If you wish to see me in person, I work out of LifeQual Center in Beaverton, Oregon.

CHAPTER 2

Angela Ambrosia

Please tell us about your company here:

LoveandRelationshipCoach.com offers Transformed Relationships, a six month at-home program. This is about writing the love story you've dreamed of living. This is about healing the hurts that have kept your relationships stuck in repeating negative patterns. This is about building the greatest relationship of all: the one with yourself. Through one-on-one coaching and a six month at-home program called Transformed Relationships, coach Angela Ambrosia will guide you through the ocean of emotions to find the person who has always already been there, intact and loving. On the other side you will find a freedom to create and a freedom to relate you may never have known.

About Angela Ambrosia:

Angela Ambrosia is a love and relationship coach with a deep affinity for women navigating unhealed hurts. She is certified as a Life Coach and relationship coach by World Coach Institute, and is a certified Subconscious Rapid Transformation Practitioner, a technique of subconscious re-patterning that transforms a person's ability to create the relationship of their dreams. Adding to her gifts of insight and affinity are her certification as a teacher of meditation, and two decades-long expertise in dance and body movement.

What is a Life Coach, and what do you do?

A life coach is professional who helps individuals see and understand who they are so they can create the changes in their life that help them experience their full potential and success in life, relationships, finances and health.

My coaching focuses intimately on how we experience love and how we feel love in ourselves: our body, our feelings and our relationships. My coaching program, Transformed Relationships, educates people to understand how love works for them so they can make the best choices in their love relationships, whether that be an intimate relationship or with those they wish to create loving relationships with in their families or larger community. We are not taught what love is or what love looks like, feels like or how it operates for us. My coaching provides the processes to understand your unique relationship to love and yourself, so you can create self-awareness about your emotions, your body and self-love, and then go on to create relationships that are mutually supportive to yourself and your loved ones.

Why would someone need a Life Coach?

Often, school, society and our families don't educate and empower us to face life challenges. A life coach can show you how to find solutions to common life problems. They give you tools to enhance your thinking and creative skills so you can learn better ways to face life challenges and overcome overwhelm or a sense that you don't know what to do.

Life coaching is an essential support system to handle and transition through obstacles such as relationship break-up, grief, addiction, communication disorders, insecurity, apathy, body issues and life transitions such as career change, moving home and losing family closeness or proximity. In modern culture, we are expected to do things by ourselves, which goes against our ancestral roots where the individual was supported by their family or 'tribe' or community.

There is an increasing need for people to refer to a Life Coach to open their eyes to the possibilities of reconnecting to the resources within themselves and their community and help individuals recover from this increasing isolation and self-dependency where they cannot seem to move forward or create the love and the life that will be truly fulfilling for them.

How do I select a Life Coach?

You need to listen to your gut about choosing a Life Coach. There are plenty of great coaches out there. So when you're listening to the coach, what do you feel intuitively and what do you think about their credentials or experience? Coaching is an interpersonal relationship, so you need to be able to identify with your coach's personality and approach. If you want someone to help you with your relationships, then you best go to someone who has a lot of experience dealing with different relationships because they can understand your unique position. Look for someone who 'speaks' your language in terms of how you think, feel and understand the world and sounds like they have been 'further down the road' to where you find yourself now.

How does coaching work?

Most coaching is done over the phone to ask questions to open you to realize the goal you are desiring and what stops you from getting those goals. At the end of every coaching session the client walks away with action steps and a new awareness of how to take action in their life, with real life tools to manage their thoughts, emotions and actions. The client agrees to commit to taking these action steps between sessions so that they can immediately implement changes to move them in a direction that betters their life. The client may need a minimum of 6 to 12 months of sessions to fully realize the changes they create with a coach. Over 6 months to a year, the client can experience how effective the action steps are and see if the changes in their life have taken root. Coaching is not a 'quick-fix' solution; it's about making permanent life changes.

How much does Life Coaching typically cost?

Per hour, coaching can cost anywhere from one hundred to three hundred to thousands of dollars for high-end or celebrity coaching. Coaches starting out offer discounts. Life coaching is for personal clients so it tends to be in the one hundred to two hundred dollar range, whereas business and executive coaching starts at the three hundred dollar mark.

What happens during a coaching session?

Typically, you have a 45min to an hour session with a coach wherein the questions asked reveal obstacles and devise solutions to the obstacles so that by the end of the call you have definitive action steps to start practicing and doing in your everyday life.

The coach brainstorms with their client and uses strategies and questions to activate the creative thought process of the client so they can start finding solutions for themselves and discover hidden talents, shift their perception of themselves and their situation and create a stronger definition of the self so they can make more effective decisions and choices. The coaching questions are typically open-ended so the client is doing most of the talking. Some coaches also share special tools that advance their clients' ability to think and understand themselves. These tools can also be worked on between sessions or through coaching programs where the client practices new life and thought habits that actually change or resolve the negative behaviors that hold them back in life.

What are your areas of specialty?

My specialty is understanding and transforming the underlying emotional and unconscious blocks that create the limiting behaviors in our relationships. Most people want to be happy. My success has been in finding the unresolved hurt inside my clients that creates their insecurity, dysfunctional relationships, self-denial, addiction, and other disruptive emotional habits. With over two decades of experience with body connection techniques, I have a deep understanding of how the body holds on to emotion and how these emotions block our higher brain function and higher emotional function.

My technique accesses the conscious, subconscious and unconscious mind, so I find where in the body and emotions the person has unresolved feelings. The tools I have reprogram the person to resolve the charges connected to the feelings and create a new relationship to their emotions so that the emotions do not take over the other parts of themselves, but rather they can manage their emotions and appreciate the knowledge that the emotions are bringing them.

I specialize in relationship break-ups, conflict or hurt in relationships, divorce, heartache, body image problems, women's insecurity, emotional imbalance, overwhelming emotions, sexual abuse recovery, sexual guilt or insecurity, intimacy issues, attracting the 'wrong' partner in relationships, inability to find a love relationship, addiction, self-hate, loneliness, major life transitions including nervous breakdown, coming of age, menopause, inability to accept a new child, pregnancy, and difficulty in parenting or handling teenagers.

What do you go over in the first session?

You can't get anywhere without a vision of where you are going. In the first session I work with the client on their unique vision for their life and relationships. This is vital for the client as they must also believe that the vision is important and have an emotional connection to it, otherwise we don't have the emotional power to get us to their dream or goal.

How long are the coaching sessions, and how often should I go?

Typical coaching sessions are 45 minutes. I prefer one hour and one hour and fifteen minute sessions as I can go deeper into the emotions and unconscious of the client. I recommend at least 6 months of coaching sessions. The frequency will depend on the coaching strategy and techniques. My techniques are more effective because of the tools I share with clients to use at home between sessions.

What are the benefits of having a Life Coach?

Firstly, with a coach, you have someone who will support you to be the best person you can be. The Life Coach is like your cheer leader, your mom, your mentor, your friend, your ally, your resource and sometimes they can play the role of a boss who calls you to do more than you think you can or want to do. Often we limit ourselves because we were raised to think we can't be more than what society, parents or school taught us. Sometimes the limits we place on ourselves are so unconscious we don't even know they are there! A Life Coach brings to light what you cannot see by yourself and helps you grow into the person that you were born to be and beyond what your limitations, society, family or world may tell you is possible.

How can I tell if a Life Coach is any good?

Read their testimonials and see what change they created for their clients and see if this is the change you are looking for. Many coaches are trained in specific techniques or skills that will be of help to you, so check out if you are interested in the particular skills the coach is sharing. For example, I have over two decades of experience in dance, movement and meditation to connect to the body, so a lot of my clients are looking for that expertise to help them connect more naturally to their body and emotions. Some people want their coach to be certified because it ensures that the coach has been taught the core ethics of coaching. However, ultimately, you want to know your coach has helped other people and they enjoyed the coach's style. I am a certified coach and I teach with a coaching school that is ICF certified. The ICF ensures a coach is working within the guidelines that keep coaching in alignment with global professional guidelines and keeps everything shared in a session confidential and secure.

How long must I commit to working with a coach?

I recommend a minimum of 6 months to see lasting and permanent change in your life. Of course, if you are getting benefits with a coach, then stay longer with the coach to keep that support system in your life that keeps you growing.

Can I hire a life coach for a short-term, special project?

It's more than possible to have a short-term coaching agreement. Sometimes you need an 'injection in the arm' from a coaching session to give you a new way of looking at things or a creative solution that the coach can provide and this can be given in one or two sessions. If I am working on the emotions and subconscious and unconscious of the person, I don't recommend the short-term approach as deep subconscious and unconscious change to emotional patterns requires practice over time. Neuroscience research has shown that changing behaviors that are rooted at the emotional level takes longer and you need to get to the source of the programming that created the negative behavior. In my experience, the best change in my clients comes from working over the longer term with committed practice to the new behavior that literally 're-wires' their body and emotions.

Why would people who are already successful hire a Life Coach?

Often, successful people will have a feeling that things could be better, or they may have one area of their life that's not as successful as they would like it to be. A coach can make the client reach their full potential so that success flows through all areas of their life. In my experience, I have found that, no matter how successful the person is, if their relationships are suffering, they are still not feeling successful or they feel something is missing in their life, almost like a spiritual emptiness. Successful relationships are the key to feeling successful in all parts of your life. Deeper meaning in life comes from being connected to others, experiencing happiness and sensing our part in creating freedom, success and joy for and with others.

Do you offer coaching remotely, either online or over the phone, or do you only see local clients?

Yes, I am based in New York City and often go 'down under' to Australia. My coaching is mostly done over phone and Skype and I hold live workshops and classes in New York City. I specialize in over-the-phone and Skype coaching as the subconscious and unconscious re-patterning techniques work better with the person when they are listening to the voice of their own mind and body and my voice.

Please tell us how readers can get in contact with you here:

Email: Angela@loveandrelationshipcoach.com or
Phone: 347 985 9979.

Event: http://www.meetup.com/New-York-Spiritual-Healing-Group/

CHAPTER 3

Kerry Labendz

Please tell us about your company here:

I am a CCA certified Life Coach in private practice. I specialize in helping busy professional women create the lives they want through a practical, solution-based, action-oriented approach that emphasizes establishing an overall sense of well-being. I offer private and group coaching as well as occasional workshops on a variety of topics. I am available for bespoke speaking engagements.

What is a Life Coach, and what do you do?

A Life Coach is similar to any other type of coach, really. Coaching is about taking you from where you are now to where you want to be. I am someone who helps you to assess your current situation, take stock of your strengths, identify areas for improvement, and develop a customized plan to achieve your goals. I support your efforts, offer an objective opinion and perspective, and serve as an accountability partner and sounding board. We work together to keep you on track and moving forward.

Why would someone need a Life Coach?

Working with a Life Coach can help you to assess your life goals and develop an action plan. Many people work with a Life Coach when they find themselves in a transitional period—they are either seeking something new or something new has already sought them out. Perhaps there is a difficult situation to be addressed or some life choices to be made. A Life Coach can help you sort through all of your options and will use proven coaching techniques to help you examine the situation and figure out the best options and choices for you. A Life Coach can also help you create a balance between your work and the rest of your life. Your Life Coach will partner with you to address and improve any area of your life that you'd like to work on.

Your Life Coach will work with you in whatever way works best for you—do you need someone to be your own personal cheerleader, or someone to kick your butt? Your Life Coach can help you strategize, support you while work through your plan and can help you get out of your own way. Life Coaching is about you and what you want to achieve.

How do I select a Life Coach?

Selecting the right Life Coach *for you* is vitally important. There are many online directories available in which you can search for Life Coaches, often by your category of interest (health and wellness, relationship coach, etc.). I recommend looking for a Life Coach who has a certification from an

ICF-accredited coaching program. Certification shows that the Life Coach has appropriate training and has committed to, signed, and is governed by a code of ethics.

Most Life Coaches offer complimentary consultations, which I highly recommend taking advantage of before you schedule an appointment. A complimentary consultation should include a mini-coaching session so that you can see what it is like to work with that person as your Life Coach. It also gives you an opportunity to ask any questions that you have about the coaching process and the coach's credentials. Talk to as many coaches as you need to until you find someone with whom you feel comfortable. You are going to be working very closely with this person, it is important that you have a good feeling about them.

How does coaching work?

Coaching is a co-creative relationship. Coaching is about assessing where you are now and figuring out how to get you to where you want to go. We work together to assess your present situation, develop a clear picture of any changes that you'd like to make and concisely define your goals. I then assist you with creating a customized plan to move you forward. As you work through your plan, I support your efforts, offer an outside perspective, and serve as an accountability partner and sounding board. We work together to keep you on track and moving forward.

I will help you to choose the best way for you to achieve what you want to achieve, while providing you with my honest coaching opinions; however, our coaching relationship is always based on your agenda, not mine. I listen, reflect, ask questions, provide perspective and opinions. I support you to find and foster your own integrity and I believe that you always know what is really best for you. You are the expert on you.

How much does Life Coaching typically cost?

Coaching costs vary widely based on location and on the background or experience of the coach. They also depend on what services you are seeking from a coach. Most Life Coaches, myself included, have several options available from single sessions to packages of multiple sessions at discounted rates, to premium coaching packages. You will be able to find a Life Coach at whatever rate you are comfortable with, though I caution you to look for certified Life Coaches and to keep in mind that you aren't paying for the coaching sessions *per se*, you are paying for solutions that will improve your life.

What happens during a coaching session?

During a coaching session we talk about your goals, dreams, and aspirations. By the end of the first coaching session we will have created 'homework' for you to complete by the time of our next session. At all subsequent sessions we discuss what you have achieved between sessions, what worked and what didn't. We will identify any obstacles that got in the way of you completing your intended goals and discuss strategies to tackle those obstacles going forward. We find a way to go over, under, around or straight through the things that are getting in your way. By the end of each session we will have identified your next steps forward and come to an agreement about what you will have accomplished by the time we meet for our next session.

What are your areas of specialty?

I specialize in helping busy professional women create the lives they want through a practical, solution-based, action-oriented approach that emphasizes establishing an overall sense of well-being. I have a holistic approach in that I believe that if any one area of your life is out of balance, it throws everything else off kilter as well. My clients tend to have several goals and dreams and typically work toward more than one at a time. The most common areas that I help my clients with are:

- **Career** – Deciding whether to change jobs or change careers, setting meaningful career goals, progressing along a fulfilling career.

- **Finance** – Creating plans to eliminate debt and increase savings.

- **Health** – Establishing healthy habits such as getting to the gym more often, finding exercise that is fun and motivating, improving nutrition, pursuing a healthy body image, and effectively coping with illness or injury.

- **Relationships** – Building more satisfying relationships with significant others, friends, family members, colleagues and coworkers. Starting to date again.

What do you go over in the first session?

In your first session we go over what it is that you hope to achieve by working with me as your Life Coach, what your goals are and what you have already done to work toward achieving them. I will want to know a little about your history and background so that I can understand the environment within which you operate on a daily basis. By the end of the first session, we will have developed an initial plan and you will be ready to take identified actions before our next session.

How long are the coaching sessions, and how often should I go?

Coaching sessions are typically 50 minutes to 1 hour long and are scheduled on a weekly basis. In some cases, sessions are scheduled every other week or even once a month. I recommend that my clients schedule sessions weekly or every other week because I find that momentum is often lost if too much time elapses between sessions.

What are the benefits of having a Life Coach?

There are many reasons why someone may not be reaching their goals, fulfilling their dreams or achieving their aspirations and could benefit from some outside assistance. We all get in our own way from time to time. Working with a Life Coach can give you a different perspective and open you up to techniques that you may not have tried or known about before. We all have our blind spots and a Life Coach can help you adjust your side and rear-view mirrors accordingly. More importantly, a coaching session is a time to focus exclusively on you, what you want and how to move you forward. That scheduled time to concentrate, with support, on your goals and dreams can make all the difference.

How can I tell if a Life Coach is any good?

If a Life Coach isn't any good, you'll know it! A good Life Coach will make you work and will challenge you in a way that makes you feel excited and energized.

How long must I commit to working with a coach?

This varies from coach to coach. I recommend that you commit yourself to the coaching process for at least 3 months (or 12 weekly sessions) if you want to see real results. Bigger goals and life changes may take longer and if you have specific short-term goals they may take less time.

Can I hire a Life Coach for a short-term, special project?

You can absolutely hire a Life Coach for a short-term or special project. My job as a Life Coach is to support my clients as they work toward their goals and dreams, whether those are short- or long-term. In fact, a short-term or special project may particularly benefit from having a coach on board to keep you focused and moving forward while you're on a tight schedule.

Why would people who are already successful hire a Life Coach?

I think that professional athletes have already answered this question. Someone who is already successful still benefits from having someone to support them while they work to achieve even more. It also helps to have an objective opinion and an extra set of eyes assessing your strengths, weaknesses, and areas that can be improved. A Life Coach will help you push yourself even further. If you are already successful, imagine how much further you can go.

Do you offer coaching remotely, either online or over the phone, or do you only see local clients?

I offer the option of in-person coaching sessions for those clients who are located in NYC, but I also coach via phone and Skype for those times that an in-person session is not convenient to schedule and for people who are located outside of New York City.

Please tell us how readers can get in contact with you here:

I can be contacted via email: Kerry@KerryLabendz.com or

Phone: 212-281-5949.

My website also has links to my Twitter, Facebook, Google+, and LinkedIn profiles, please visit www.KerryLabendz.com for more information.

CHAPTER 4

Grant M. Ingle, PhD

Please tell us about your company here:

I'm an organizational psychologist who provides coaching to people in leadership positions in the private, public and non-profit sectors, primarily in New England and New York. In addition, I serve as an external advisor to large change projects concerned with changing behavior or improving organizational climate and culture.

What is a Leadership Coach, and what do you do?

A leadership coach provides assistance to people in leadership positions regarding what they want to accomplish and how. I approach leadership coaching by focusing on the impact and effectiveness of a leader's behavior and how that behavior shapes that of others as well as organizational culture and climate.

I'm already pretty successful. Why would I need a Leadership Coach?

'Pretty successful' leaders often hire a leadership coach so that they can become 'very successful' leaders. It's common practice to conduct a 360 developmental assessment at the beginning of a coaching engagement to identify areas to address in coaching. The client identifies 12-14 people in their work environment who will be interviewed by the coach to answer two questions: (1) what does the client do very well? and (2) what two or three things could the client do to further improve his or her effectiveness and leadership impact? Interviewees include direct reports, peers and a boss and/or board members. After conducting the interviews, the leadership coach writes a report that summarizes the client's strengths and development opportunities. This report is shared first with the client, then with the boss or board, and finally is discussed in a joint meeting of the two to set priorities for the development opportunities. In my experience, even very successful leaders are unaware of shortcomings in their skills or inconsistent or conflicting behavior that makes them less effective than they could be. These shortcomings will be evident to others in the work environment, and will emerge as themes in the 360 interviews. In this way the 360 assessment provides an initial benchmark regarding areas for improvement that need to be addressed through coaching.

How do I select a Leadership Coach?

Choosing a leadership coach who's a good fit for you isn't difficult. Search online for both local and national listings of coaches in your geographic area and also ask your friends and colleagues for referrals. Narrow your search to two to five coaches and review their websites to get a sense of their style of coaching and specialties. Almost all coaches provide a complimentary initial consultation of 20 to 60 minutes. Why?

Because coaches want their clients to be a good fit for them as well. If the fit clearly isn't a good one, most coaches will refer you to other coaches who might be more appropriate.

Make sure to prepare in advance for your conversation with a prospective coach:

- Be able to clearly describe the specific issue, situation or opportunity you want to address in coaching, what you want to accomplish and in what time span.

- Indicate early on if you are looking for coaching on the phone, in-person coaching or a mix of both; many coaches prefer to travel to meet a client for an in-person session early on and then continue the coaching by phone with periodic in-person sessions.

- Be clear about whether you or your company will be paying for the coaching (company coaching rates are usually higher than those for individuals; rates also differ between public, private and non-profit sectors and can vary considerably by geographic location).

- Understand that leadership coaches are professionals who will have rates similar to those of other professionals you hire like lawyers or tax accountants.

- Be prepared to ask the coach about his or her past coaching experience and their credentials; most coaches will gladly send you their resume; also check them out on LinkedIn and other business social media.

Once you've narrowed down your list of prospective coaches, make an appointment to speak on the phone with the coach that seems most appropriate. Let the coach know what your search process is (i.e., that you've got a short list and are interviewing them so see who might be the best fit, etc.). Remember to take notes. If the first coach you call seems to be a good fit it's your choice whether to call the others or not.

If you'd like to proceed with this first coach, ask what their policy is regarding a complimentary session. Also ask about rates and how they typically work with clients. Most coaches prefer to meet directly with clients early in the coaching relationship and some prefer in-person sessions, so also inquire about the coach's approach to in-person versus phone sessions. Some coaches will offer this complimentary session on the spot if they have time, while others prefer to schedule it in the near future. If you have any doubts after the session, set up a call with the next coach on your list. In any event, do send a follow up email to any coach you spoke with but didn't choose, thanking them for their time… You never know when you might cross paths again…

What sort of topics would you coach me about?

In my practice, the topics for coaching are client-driven, not determined by me. Clients often seek out a leadership coach due to an initial challenging issue or issues that have arisen in their work life.

In my experience, common issues can include:

- Conflict with a direct report, a peer, boss or board member(s)

- Wanting to improve a particular area such as team leadership or communication skills

- Concerns about how to improve an increasingly negative work environment

- Improving impact and effectiveness as a leader after a major shortcoming

- Assistance sorting through the implications of a reorganization or change in role

- Concerns about taking on a major project for which she or he doesn't feel adequately supported

- Help thinking through decisions to stay or leave a position or to seek a promotion

- Assistance responding to negative developments in large change projects

- Understanding organizational resistance to change and exploring steps to counter it

- Support and strategies for improving organizational work climate following an incident

- Assistance in better managing the activities and tone of dysfunctional board committees

- Help in developing engagement agreements for a team with conflicting work styles

- Developing a strategy for breaking down the silos in a leader's organization

While issues that bring clients to coaching can be related to addressing a negative issue or experience, there are often positive reasons for engaging a coach as well:

- Clients who have resolved a past issue or problem through coaching often come to see coaching as an ongoing approach for enhancing their leadership

- A new CEO has asked all members of the senior management team to consider leadership coaching to improve their individual and group effectiveness

- A newly promoted client wants assistance from a coach in taking on the new role

- A promising opportunity has emerged that a client wants to think through with a coach

- A client wants to explore how best to approach and roll out a complex project

- A team wants the support of a coach to further improve its process of working together

- An executive director seeks assistance developing a more collaborative work environment

- HR introduces a new menu of optional leadership development activities that include coaching

- A successful client wants to further improve his or her leadership style with direct reports

- A newly hired senior leadership team member has negotiated for ongoing coaching support as part of her compensation package

How much does Leadership Coaching typically cost?

The cost of leadership coaching ranges considerably by geographic region, sector and whether the client is paying directly for coaching or the company is paying. In the New York City metropolitan area, leadership coaching for private sector clients paid for by the company can be as much as $1000 per hour. In rural areas, leadership coaches can charge as little as $100 per hour.

What happens during a coaching session?

Typically, the client and the leadership coach have agreed on specific areas to address early on in the coaching relationship. A typical coaching session begins with reviewing what has transpired since the last session and then transitions into joint work on the agreed-upon areas. Toward the end of the session, discussion turns to next steps the client will take, and these will be reviewed at the beginning of the next session. This approach accelerates change because of the accountability built into the coaching relationship and its regular sessions.

What are your areas of specialty?

My areas of specialty include: (1) addressing issues of behavior on the part of clients and that of others in the work environment that are having a negative impact on the work environment; and (2) addressing issues related to improving organizational climate and culture. Both can include reducing the incidence of unwanted or negative behavior such as bullying, or increasing the incidence of positive and desirable behaviors such as cross-functional collaboration.

What do you go over in the first session?

In the first session I reiterate what I heard from the new client in the complimentary session regarding his or her goals for coaching and the time frame for accomplishing them. If not covered in the previous session, I also review my policies regarding cancellation of sessions, confidentiality, and also make clear that I don't bill for conversations under 15 minutes between sessions if a client has a quick question or needs to check in briefly.

How long are the coaching sessions, and how often should I go?

Most leadership coaching occurs in two hour-long sessions per month; though this is largely determined by the client's needs and wishes. For example, some clients want more frequent coaching initially and choose to have weekly sessions for the first month or two before transitioning to two sessions per month. In my experience, coaching sessions that are held less than twice a month tend to be unproductive, because there is an inadequate level of engagement between the client and the coach.

What are the benefits of having a Leadership Coach?

The benefits of this coaching approach for my clients include initial relief about having one-on-one professional support and a confidential forum for discussing necessary changes, gaining new perspectives and insights about their options, and growing confidence as clients put desired changes in place.

How can I tell if a Leadership Coach is any good?

A coach could be very good as a coach in general terms, but nonetheless a poor match for you. Beyond examining the coach's credentials, endorsements, website and social media, the question of whether a coach is 'good' is very client-dependent. Make sure to take advantage of the free initial session that is offered by most leadership coaches to see if the fit seems right to you. Here are some ways to assess your first session with a coach:

- You're put at ease by the coach and feel comfortable talking with her or him

- The coach understands what you'd like to accomplish and asks thoughtful questions.

- Your conversation with the coach has already started to give you new insights, ideas or perspectives

- You feel energized, optimistic and also relieved about getting help in moving forward

- The coach has experience coaching others at your level of leadership and in the same or a similar industry or sector

How long must I commit to working with a coach?

Usually leadership coaches prefer an initial three or six month engagement at the end of which progress is assessed, priorities are reviewed, and a decision to continue the coaching relationship or not is revisited. In my own experience, significant change in personal behavior usually takes about six months to establish. Changing team or workgroup behavior takes at least a year to know if the change has taken hold. Efforts to improve organizational climate usually take at least two years to have demonstrated impact.

Can I hire a leadership coach for a short-term, special project?

Yes, but be clear who the client is — you, the project or both. Competent coaches faced with such a request will usually raise this question of who the client is. The way this question is answered establishes the coach's priorities and defines what the goals are for the coaching engagement.

What qualifies you to coach me? I'm an Executive/CEO/President of my organization.

You're the specialist when it comes to your organization and its management, but a coach is a specialist when it comes to coaching leaders. I've been a practicing organizational psychologist (not an academic) and leadership coach for over 30 years.

Do you offer coaching remotely, either online or over the phone, or do you only see local clients?

The answer to this question is usually jointly decided by the client and the coach. I prefer to meet with clients in person early on in the engagement and then move to phone sessions, though I like to meet with clients in person periodically, usually quarterly. However, I have some distant clients whom I have never met and others who prefer meeting in person.

Please tell us how readers can get in contact with you here:

Email: leadershipcoach2@gmail.com

Phone: 413.274.8088

Web site: leadershipcoach2.com

CHAPTER 5

Kellee Tyler

Please tell us about your company here:

A Goal Achieved, LLC. is an up and coming personal services organization. Established in 2014, this company focuses on the needs of the client. Confidentiality is our promise to the client.

A completely online/audio service provides the convenience and anonymity most clients seek. A Goal Achieved, LLC. is committed to helping the client achieve their goals, dreams, and desires. A Life Coach is a co-partner in the client's journey to success.

What is a Life Coach, and what do you do?

A Life Coach is like a cheerleader for life. We all need someone on our side to help us reach our potential. A Life Coach meets with the client to provide support and honest objectivity to aid in motivating the client to achieve their goal, dreams, and desires. The coach offers another perspective to the approach the client is applying to reach his/her potential. A Life Coach aids in exploring new ideas to achieve what the client seeks to do.

Why would someone need a Life Coach?

We often desire things in our life but are self-defeating. We may have negative reflection on what it will take to achieve our goal. We may have run out of ideas to get to the destination. We lose momentum along the way to our dream. We think we can't have what we want. A coach provides the support and positive perspective to the client's approach. Someone who suffers these symptoms simply needs a partner to walk the path to success. Everything is easier with the Buddy system.

How do I select a Life Coach?

The Life Coach selected should be certified by an accredited educator. They should be recognized as a member in good standing with the Certified Coaching Allegiance. The coach should be specialized.

How does coaching work?

The process is based specifically on the needs of the client. I use a 4-srep process: *Examined, Imagine, Action, and Achieve.*

- **Examine** - Determine where the client is in their life today in relation to where they want to be, a starting point.

- **Imagine** - Determine where the client wants to be, a destination.

- **Action** - Determine how to get the client to where he/ she wants to go, a plan.

- **Achieve** - Reach the goals and desired result, A Goal Achieved.

How much does Life Coaching typically cost?

Coaching can cost as little as $50 per session to upwards of $500 per session.

What happens during a coaching session?

There are many different approaches to the coaching sessions. In general, the coach and client meet to determine the client's goals, dreams, and desires. During scheduled meetings the coach and client develop an approach to achieve what the client seeks. Milestones are established. The hurdles are identified and solutions found. Victories are celebrated along the way.

What are your areas of specialty?

I am a Certified Transformation Coach. This means I work with people who are looking to transform their lives. It may be a person coming out of divorce or experiencing loss of a loved one. It may be a career change. Basically, anyone desiring to change their life circumstances or recover from a life-changing event.

What do you go over in the first session?

The first session is always used to determine whether the client truly needs coaching and what the expectations are on both sides of the equation. A price package and schedule of meetings is established. There is a brief discussion of the goals, dreams, and desires. The client leaves with homework to prepare for the next meeting.

How long are the coaching sessions, and how often should I go?

This is truly based on the practice of the coach. Most sessions are anywhere from 45 minutes to 1 ½ hours, it depends on the coach. The frequency of sessions is also determined by the coach and the needs of the client. It may be weekly or twice a month. In some cases there has been a need for biweekly sessions or possibly only a monthly meeting.

What are the benefits of having a Life Coach?

Simply put, to achieve goals, dreams, and desires. We don't have to go it alone. It is like playing a game of rummy. The client has all the cards but may be blind to a winning strategy. This is where the coach comes in, to help the client develop a winning strategy to achieve the desired destination.

How can I tell if a Life Coach is any good?

This is truly by personal experience. If the client feels he/she is getting the attention they need and feel good about themselves and their dreams when they leave then it is a successful relationship.

How long must I commit to working with a coach?

Most situations call for 8 - 10 weeks' commitment, but many clients discover other desires while working within the program and will extend the contract.

Can I hire a life coach for a short-term, special project?

Yes, most coaches will commit to a short-term commitment, but some have a minimum session requirement.

Why would people who are already successful hire a life coach?

Everyone has something they wish to achieve but have been unable to get there on their own.

Do you offer coaching remotely, either online or over the phone, or do you only see local clients?

I do not see local clients. All my sessions are by phone or email, and group sessions are available.

Please tell us how readers can get in contact with you here:

Email: agoalachieved@acoachisneeded.com

Contact Number: 757-288-7474

CHAPTER 6

Jalaal Aleem Madyun

Please tell us about your company here:

J AM Life Coaching specializes in helping people build romantic relationships with substance. For singles seeking a relationship, you'll learn how to attract quality dating options in a way that feels natural. You'll learn to build confidence in your ability to approach and meet new people. You'll learn how to break the cycle of dating the same type of person that ultimately goes nowhere. You'll learn to bounce back from past relationships and start dating from a place of personal confidence and meaning.

For people who are already in relationships, you'll learn how to keep the bond rock solid. This means curing the conflict so that you can avoid arguments, adding spark into the relationship so it doesn't feel like you are going through the motions and gaining clarity on whether it is time to take it to the next level (e.g. marriage) or potentially end the relationship.

What is a Life Coach, and what do you do?

Coaches help you establish measurable goals, create action plans and break them down into achievable steps. Life Coaching is for people who want to get the most out of life. They are ready and willing to improve so that they can achieve certain goals in life. That might mean that they want to overcome a habit that is holding them back or they want to gain a specific skillset.

The title of the field says it all. "Life Coaching" touches on every area of life. For that reason, coaches are usually trained with a versatile skillset so they can handle a variety of issues. Many coaches choose to specialize in a specific area, but the foundational principles of Life Coaching still apply.

Coaches are focused on the present rather than the past and they work with people who are mentally healthy and fully functioning.

Why would someone need a Life Coach?

When you have an important goal that requires accountability, support and productive challenges, a coach is your best bet to get you there. People hire coaches because they want another perspective that they can trust to bring new possibilities into their awareness. They are usually very successful people who realize the value of being held accountable by a neutral source and having someone who will stick with you through the rough patches until you accomplish your goals. Coaches increase your effectiveness and overall morale without dictating terms to you or demanding anything that makes you unreasonably uncomfortable. A coach combines their expertise with your intuition to figure out your 'secret sauce' to success and how you can perform at your peak on a continuous basis.

How do I select a Life Coach?

To find a coach, you just have to do a little homework. If you have a good network that you trust, start with asking if anyone else has worked with a coach and had success. A trusted referral is always solid.

Of course, your friendly neighborhood search engine, Google, can point you in the right direction. Proximity matters to most people. Having someone who is local and can meet you in person feels safe, but there are coaches all over the world who can serve your needs. Try searching for websites that feature several coaches. Use phrases such as "List of Life Coaches" or "Life Coach Directory" to find a selection of coaches to choose from.

How does coaching work?

The primary mode of coaching is a meeting over the phone, online or in person to address specific goals on a continuous basis. The real value of coaching is the conversations you have and the realizations they cause.

The most frequent structure of coaching is a one-on-one meeting in a private setting. Some coaches offer group coaching settings or even live events with large audiences.

When you find a coach, you decide collectively how long you would like to work together and what you would like to accomplish. The coach utilizes powerful questions to help you gain clarity and keep you on track for the goals you outlined.

How much does Life Coaching typically cost?

Like many things in life, the old adage, "You get what you pay for" applies to coaching. There's a vast range of experience, special expertise and services, so you have to decide what sounds the most appealing to you. I know coaches who charge by the session and others (like myself) who create packages with several services in them. The typical hourly rate for a Life Coach is around $150 an hour. Coaches who are newer or still pursuing their certification may charge significantly less, from $50 to $100 an hour. For business or executive coaches, the average hourly rate increases to around $500 an hour.

The cost of coaching packages can vary significantly. Many coaches simply allow people to purchase multiple hourly sessions at a reduced rate rather than purchasing one session at a time. Others use standard programs for a set length of time, usually 8 weeks up to 12 months, and they have several price points for those packages. A reasonable cost range for packages is $400 to $5,000 depending on the coach. There are some coaches who almost exclusively charge between $10,000 and $50,000 for their signature packages, but that range is not the norm in the coaching industry.

What happens during a coaching session?

First and foremost, a good coach will establish the goal for that particular session. If the person receiving coaching has a clear objective, then the coach will begin the process of asking questions that explore the issue comprehensively and eventually leads into exploring the options for action steps to move towards the goal. If the objective for the session is unclear, it is the coach's role to help the coachee get clear on what they would like to explore.

Human beings happen to thrive based on variety. Even the best coach will have trouble keeping the energy high and maintaining momentum if they use the exact same format with every session. That being said, there are various methods a coach may use before, during and after the session to increase inspiration.

For example, the coach may take the coachee through a guided visualization during the session or have them complete an assessment that will reveal potential areas for growth related to the goals of the session. Coaches are trained in specific methodologies that often use questionnaires or exercises to consistently and accurately pinpoint what is holding you back.

Obviously, different options are available depending on whether the session is happening over the phone, online or in person.

What are your areas of specialty?

My area of specialty is people who want to build healthy romantic relationships with substance. The majority of the people I work with are single and looking for a relationship. They usually are very confident and quite spectacular in other areas of life, but when it comes to dating and relationships, they haven't been able to crack the code. My job is to help them figure out EXACTLY what they have been doing to contribute to the past relationships that didn't work and what actions they can take now to start pursuing the types of relationships that will truly make them happy. Not everyone I coach desires a serious, monogamous relationship, but they usually want someone with whom they feel a legitimate connection.

For people in relationships, I am seen as the conflict cure. In school, we learn history, math and science, but the success principles for romantic relationships are not part of the curriculum. When two people come together with different backgrounds and ideas about the way a relationship should work, there is bound to be a clash at some point. My role is to help people in relationships to find peace and balance. I help people take control of their actions towards their partner and ultimately make a decision about whether or not they can make their current relationship work.

What do you go over in the first session?

When people seek me as a coach, they normally know what they want to change in their life. My job during the first session is to set the table for complete honesty and allow them to bring me into their world. By the end of the first session, I want to know the details about what is keeping them up at night and what they have going in their favor.

If they are not sure how to approach the conversation, I love the metaphor of a genie. I'll ask them, "If you could ask a genie 3 questions about life, dating or relationships, what would they be?" This question gets the ideas rolling and people often laugh and ask if I am sure I want to open that can of worms. During the first session, people usually have realistic expectations. My philosophy is, why stop there? I want to know what you really want, even if it feels unrealistic at the time. That's what we should be striving for! The only limitations are the ones you place on yourself.

Since I have a particular area of expertise, I usually tell them what services I offer and how they relate to their goals. I have regularly scheduled meetings with everyone I coach. For some people, I communicate daily through email or even attend live events with them to give feedback on the spot. During the first session, we'll decide which services would bring about the highest transformation.

How long are the coaching sessions, and how often should I go?

Most coaches have sessions from 30-90 minutes. While I do think it is important to have a guideline, such as 60 minutes on average, it is not the most important factor in the coaching relationship. People value the results they get from coaching, regardless of the time it takes to get there. Over the course of a few months, some of my sessions will last for 45 minutes while others will last for 2 hours. I'm not concerned with the clock nearly as much as I am concerned with delivering the value necessary for you to move forward with confidence.

A coach who is worth working with will have the same philosophy. When you decide how often you should meet with them, consider how long it takes to reach your goals during each session and whether you are good at sticking to the game plan in between sessions.

At the beginning of coaching, the meetings are typically longer and happen more frequently. As you hit a groove and gain momentum, you may start reaching your goals quicker during the session and you'll also feel that you need to meet less often. In order to be effective, most coaches will meet with you at least on a weekly basis. If you only meet with a coach once a month, that is not often enough for most people to get the full value of the coaching process. Therefore, 2 to 4 times a month is common.

What are the benefits of having a Life Coach?

The benefits of having a Life Coach are endless; namely, an improved quality of life and optimism about what is possible for you. They tap into your intuition to set the tone for an outcome that is authentic to you. The personal growth you experience is hard to measure, but you can feel it in your heart, mind and spirit when you've transformed as a person.

One of the less noticeable, but significant benefits of hiring a coach is that there is no stigma attached to coaching. When you tell someone that you have a counselor or a therapist, the assumption is that there is something fundamentally wrong with you. You might be judged as mentally unstable, whether that is accurate or not. With coaching, there is a positive aura around the field and you are seen as a person who is taking responsibility for achieving a higher level of success in life.

How can I tell if a Life Coach is any good?

A phrase I use often in life is "everything is relative". That means that two people can experience the exact same thing and they will have slightly different evaluations of it based on their personal criteria. If you can experience what it is like to work with the coach, you can generally trust your gut. Even if they are a skilled and experienced coach, that doesn't automatically mean they are the best coach for YOU.

It's like a taste test. I can place several delicious looking desserts on a table for you to try. All of them look appealing in their own way, but you won't know which one is the best until you have had a chance to sample them.

If a coach offers a complimentary introductory session, take it. In addition, some websites are actually dedicated to collecting information on coaches and providing you with recommendations.

Here are a few questions you may want to ask yourself:

- Do they present themselves in a professional manner?

- Do they have testimonials?

- How do I feel about their communication style?

- Are they focused on helping me or touting their accomplishments?

- Are they trying to sell or pressure me to hire them or do they respect my right to choose?

- Does their expertise or programs address my most important concerns?

Trust your intuition. Listen to what your gut is saying about whether you feel like you would get closer to reaching your goals while you are coaching with them.

How long must I commit to working with a coach?

Before you decide to work with a coach, you need to establish 'coachable goals'. That simply means that there is a measure of success that can be easily identified. For me, the measure of success can be a single person who enters into an exclusive relationship. Depending on your needs, you might want to identify a specific project you're working on, a decision you need to make, or a goal you want to accomplish. For the best results, you should plan to work with the coach until you reach your goal.

At that point, you can decide whether to create new goals and continue or end the coaching relationship. Some coaches allow you to pay a monthly fee for the option to have a check-in.

My personal stance is that the coach shouldn't mandate that you commit to a long-term timeframe. Based on their experience, the coach will help you set expectations around what a realistic timeframe is to accomplish the goal, but the choice is yours. You're going to be the one who has to take action on a consistent basis.

Can I hire a life coach for a short-term, special project?

Short-term projects are fairly common, especially for Life Coaches who work with businesses. Typically, if you work with a coach on a special project, there is a clear deadline for accomplishing the goal and the urgency is higher than normal. An example would be an assignment at work that requires focus and dedicated action for the next month. In dating and relationship coaching, I work with people based on a short-term transition or a challenge. For example, they are moving out of state with their partner in 3 weeks and want to keep the chemistry in their relationship in tact during the hectic move, or they have entered into a program to lose weight over the next 30 days and want a coach to help them stay motivated to increase their attractiveness.

Why would people who are already successful hire a life coach?

The International Coaching Federation (ICF), along with several other entities, has conducted studies that show the return on investment (ROI) for coaching is extremely high. It is because coaching increases accountability and helps to create awareness about the action steps necessary to get to the next level. Success is not a static thing that never changes. As you advance in your career, relationships, family life and even recreation, you'll notice that what got you to this level won't necessarily carry you to the next. If you aren't working with a coach, chances are that someone you'll have to compete with IS working with a coach and their development is likely progressing at a faster rate.

Success has several components. You can feel successful overall, but are you performing at your absolute peak in every area? If you are an executive who receives awards for your performance, is there room for improvement with your time management skills, your leadership qualities, your ability to relate to those you manage, your vision for the company or your consistency for producing results? When I coach people, I look at their external features, their internal qualities and their interactions with other people. I have yet to meet a perfect human being (and I try to dissuade those I coach from expecting perfection). However, progress is worthwhile and there are likely several ways a successful person can become even better.

Do you offer coaching remotely, either online or over the phone, or do you only see local clients?

I offer coaching online, over the phone and in person with people who are local. I've found that the coaching session is effective in either method for different reasons.

Over the phone, people tend to be very blunt and honest because they don't have to be nervous about watching my reaction. They share very intimate details. That is great for me as a coach because I can get real results based on real conversation.

Online, you have the benefit of being in a comfortable environment, such as your home, and we have the added benefit of using visual communication. In person, the connection is built the fastest and I am able to pick up on your energy and use eye contact and body language to add emphasize my statements.

Periodically, I will travel out of state to meet in person with people I coach. I believe in making myself available in whichever method makes the most sense and has the biggest impact.

Please tell us how readers can get in contact with you here:

Visit www.JAMLifeCoaching.com for information on my services, more resources or to contact me directly.

Consider me a trusted advisor. The lines of communication are always open.

CHAPTER 7

Iris Fanning

Please tell us about your company here:

I am one of the early adopters of coaching. I attended and graduated from Coach University, a 2 year accredited coaching program. I've owned my coaching business for the past 15 years. I've worked with a variety of clients and found my niche. I coach intelligent, successful women who want coaching in a variety of areas including: work/life balance; leadership; employee motivation; work promotion; dealing with colleague conflicts; getting ahead financially; finding love; mastering new skills; goal setting.

What is a Life Coach, and what do you do?

A Life Coach is a trained professional who has training, experience and skills to assist people to make the most of their lives. When I coach, the focus is always on my client's needs, focus, wants and desires. Through a variety of exercises, deep questions, fieldwork, and interaction, I help clients move forward faster with more ease and have more fun.

Why would someone need a Life Coach?

There are a variety of reasons for someone to want or need

to work with a Life Coach. There are dozens of coaching specialties including wellness; relationships; work/life balance; leadership; executive; retirement; spirituality etc.

How do I select a Life Coach?

I would advise each person to look into the credentials of the coach. After that, the person needs to feel a connection and believe they can work well with the coach. There are many coaching styles ranging from more supportive yet accountable to a drill sergeant type. Depending on the person's temperament they need to choose who they can work with.

Here are some key questions to help:

1. Please tell me about your coach training and experience.

2. How long have you been a coach? What did you do before you were a coach?

3. What do your clients say about you?

4. What is the average amount of time your clients stay with you?

5. How do you handle differences with your clients?

How does coaching work?

There are coaches who do in person work and others who work via the phone or Skype. I was trained to do phone coaching so that my clients can live all over the United States and Canada. In either case, the client and coach work together typically weekly, anywhere from 30-90 minutes. Most coaches assign field work to do in between calls. Additionally, most coaches include unlimited emails in between sessions.

How much does Life Coaching typically cost?

It's interesting, there is a huge range. I've seen coaches charge over $1000 a month and other coaches charge about $250 a month. I am convinced that more money does NOT mean better coaching. More money usually means the coach is a better marketer, not necessarily a better coach.

What happens during a coaching session?

Generally there is a follow up from the actions and fieldwork the client worked on the week prior. We talk about success and obstacles and follow up with how to get through those obstacles. Then coaching can go a variety of ways. If the client is working on a long-term project additional action items, re-framing, skill building, support, clarification, sometimes different viewpoints are all brought to the session.

Additionally, the coach often provides a program within the goals of the client such as setting stronger boundaries, raising client standards, building a strong business etc. Each session is unique and focuses on the client. There is a saying though, "The Client Does the Work." So, while the coach leads, guides and coaches (like a coach for any team), it's the individual who does the training and wins the game.

What are your areas of specialty?

I've owned my coaching business for the past 15 years. I've worked with a variety of clients and found my niche. I coach intelligent, successful women who want coaching in a variety of areas including work/life balance; leadership; employee motivation; work promotion; dealing with colleague conflicts; getting ahead financially; finding love; mastering new skills; goal setting.

What do you go over in the first session?

There are really two first sessions in my coaching. The first is a free 20 minute Discovery Session where the client and I work together. This is designed to get an overview of what the client wants to work on and expects from coaching. Additionally, it allows the client and me to get to know each other. That way the client can decide, risk free, if we are a good coaching match.

When the client decides to work with me, we then have our initial session. Prior to our call I send a lengthy Welcome Packet for them to complete. We may spend 1-3 sessions digging into that Welcome Packet. It includes goals, strengths, self-sabotage, aspirations, big dreams etc. This work then lays the foundation for what we will work together on in the upcoming months.

How long are the coaching sessions, and how often should I go?

I have found that weekly coaching sessions of 45 minutes is ideal. First, because, in that amount of time, clients become succinct in approaching what they want and how they are achieving it. More importantly, there is research that shows that at the start of any session/lesson/workshop, people are highly focused and have great concentration. Then, over time, concentration slowly goes down and then people often 'space out' at about 40 minutes. So, if we work hard and have fun during those 45 minutes, it's the perfect amount of time.

What are the benefits of having a Life Coach?

The benefits are too numerous to mention all of them. Here's just a small sampling:

1. Stronger leadership

2. Greater strategies

3. Ability to work as a team

4. Ability to create a strong team

5. Improved communication skills

6. Greater financial freedom

7. Strong work/life balance

8. Improved relationships

9. Improved health and wellness

10. Finding love

11. Setting stronger boundaries

12. Raising personal standards

13. Learning to say "No" to what you don't want

14. Learning to stop being a people pleaser

15. Celebrating successes

16. Improving your business

17. Building a strong personal foundation

18. Getting rid of toleration

19. Clarifying goals

20. Mastering new skills

How can I tell if a Life Coach is any good?

It's pretty simple. Are you moving closer to your goals? Are you achieving what you set out to achieve? Are you becoming a better you? Are you feeling supported and learning new tools and skills?

Have you noticed a better attitude in yourself and how you are being treated? Do you look forward to your coaching time?

How long must I commit to working with a coach?

I say a minimum of 3 months to see some changes toward what you want. After that it's individual and depends on how big your goals and dreams are. It can be a year or two.

Also, it's not uncommon for my clients to work a period of time, accomplish what they want, and then come back with new ideas months or years later.

Can I hire a life coach for a short-term, special project?

Most coaches are happy to work on short-term projects. Others only take pre-paid clients for long-term coaching programs.

Why would people who are already successful hire a Life Coach?

My clients are all successful! They want to go further, learn more, have support, and benefit from the coaching process.

Do you offer coaching remotely, either online or over the phone, or do you only see local clients?

I offer all my coaching via the phone and unlimited emails in between.

Please tell us how readers can get in contact with you here:

Name: Iris Fanning

Phone: 505-821-6018

Website: www.irisfanning.com

Email: coachiris@hotmail.com

CHAPTER 8

Clary Torres

Please tell us about your company here:

After 2 years of working with an executive business coach, I decided to branch out on my own, in 2010, as a personal life coach and started Clary Torres Intl. I noticed that I was attracting more personal development clients than business, and that was more fulfilling for me so I decided to make that my niche.

What is a Life Coach, and what do you do?

People use life coaches for the same reason that they use sports coaches; they want someone to work with them, to encourage them, and to push them. Most individuals know exactly what they need to do to develop healthy lifestyle habits, whether it be weight loss motivation, stress management, exercising, or following their physician's recommendations. However, actually following through and taking action, or maintaining action for a lifetime, is an ongoing struggle for many people.

It is important to understand, though, that we do not have the ability to diagnose or treat mental or health conditions. We are here to assist or support their life path.

As a life coach I explore the client's greatest concerns and goals, the obstacles to achieving those goals, and strategies to overcome the obstacles.

Why would someone need a Life Coach?

Life coaches are guides who have 'been there, done that'. If you find yourself feeling 'stuck' in any given part of your life, personal or professional, they will, basically, get you from where you are currently, to where you want to be in the most effective way. And if you are not clear as to where you want to be, you just know that you are not happy where you are at, they can help identify your life path and brighten your daily mental outlook.

How do I select a Life Coach?

What is important about finding a good coach to work with is to find the right fit for you. Your Life Coach should be someone you can connect with and feel comfortable to be able to share your personal life with, with ease. The more you open up to your life coach the better they can guide you and help you.

Before you select a Life Coach make sure you have a good conversation with them. Ask them about how they work, what to expect and share your concerns and reasons why you are looking for a Life Coach. By the end of the conversation you should feel that you made a connection and have all the information you need to make a decision.

How does coaching work?

Each coach has their own unique style and tactics, but in general coaches use a series of questions to help you identify what is holding you back, guide you and give you strategies on how to overcome obstacles and reach your goals.

How much does Life Coaching typically cost?

The range of cost can be anywhere from hundreds to thousands. It varies a lot. A few coaches offer per sessions but most offer packages.

What happens during a coaching session?

Some coaches have set programs that they follow depending on the client's needs. I personally do not have a set program. I customize my service per client for their particular goal or need. During the session we evaluate where they are in their goals and the road map that we set together. We work out strategies to overcome obstacles and give them'challenges' or 'homework' they have to accomplish during the week.

What are your areas of specialty?

My area of specialty is personal development and the law of attraction is the fundamental tool I use in my coaching. I guide you step-by-step and help you identify what it is you really want, what's preventing you from getting it, and how to break through any barriers to take action and transform your life.

What do you go over in the first session?

The first session is about getting to know each other and making sure that we are a good fit for each other. I share about me and how I like to work and what to expect and what not to expect from me. I also like to interview the person and make sure they understand what life coaching is and that it is not therapy or psychology. I find out exactly what encouraged them to look for a Life Coach and what is it that they expect to get out of the experience. If I see that we are a good fit, then I make suggestions on what service package best fits their needs.

How long are the coaching sessions, and how often should I go?

Every coach is different, but for me, a session can last anywhere from thirty minutes to an hour and a half. Sessions should be held at least weekly. But the more communication the better.

What are the benefits of having a Life Coach?

They can assess your situation, help you develop a strategy to overcome the obstacles you're facing, and provide you with support while you work through those obstacles. Whether for business or personal coaching, your relationship with a Life Coach should leave you with more self-confidence, knowledge, and a better attitude towards dealing with whatever life may throw your way.

How can I tell if a Life Coach is any good?

I think most coaches are good and have value to offer to clients. A good Life Coach will not tell you what to do or what path to take. They will guide you to find your own path. And whatever path you take, they will encourage and support you along the way until you reach your goal or you feel you no longer need their assistance.

How long must I commit to working with a coach?

Some people just want to be pointed in the right direction and this can happen from one session to one month. Others prefer to hold on to their coaches until their goal is fulfilled and, depending on what the goal is, this could mean anywhere from three months to one year or longer. For some people their relationship with their Life Coach is ongoing, depending on the complexity of their lives.

Can I hire a life coach for a short-term, special project?

Yes. Coaches are project motivated by nature so we are ready to support and encourage you all the way to the finish line.

Why would people who are already successful hire a life coach?

Some people may be very successful in one area of their lives but at the expense of another area of their lives and, because of that, they are not 100% happy. Let's say a business person is very successful in their business because they dedicated their whole life to it and wake up one day to the reality of divorce.

They do not have the tools to bring about a more fulfilling life. A Life Coach can help them bring peace and balance to their lives.

Do you offer coaching remotely, either online or over the phone, or do you only see local clients?

The beauty of the internet is that it has opened the doors for me to help people around the world from the comfort of my home office. I coach people online through chat, Facebook, Skype, phone and locally in person.

Please tell us how readers can get in contact with you here:

Website: www.ClaryTorres.com

Phone #: 407-349-7144

Email: ClaryLifeCoach@gmail.com

Facebook: Facebook.com/ClaryLifeCoach

Twitter: Twitter.com/Clary_Torres

CHAPTER 9

Nina Elisa Segura

What is a Life Coach, and what do you do?

That is a very good question. I consider myself a Life and Leadership Coach. The first step in working with clients is to help them get clarity about their own inner leader. We are all born with a part of ourselves that leads us towards the fullest expression of our life purpose.

Why would someone need a Life Coach?

Hiring a Life Coach is like hiring a personal trainer (versus hiring a physical therapist — that would be more like a mental health counselor). A professional certified Life Coach helps clients clarify their vision, set goals, align with allies, create a plan of action, reframe when things don't go as expected and sustain positive personal and professional change.

How do I select a Life Coach?

Of course trust your own inner leader. I suggest that it is someone who is certified with the International Coaching Federation and, of course, someone you can trust and look up to.

How does coaching work?

After the client has decided to choose me as their coach and has paid and signed the contract, we design how the coaching relationship will work, and then we start the discovery process, which typically includes value-based and leadership assessments. After that, see above answer to "Why would someone need a Life Coach?"

How much does Life Coaching typically cost?

Again, it is not regulated, however a good, certified Life Coach should charge no less than $100 an hour.

What happens during a coaching session?

This is based on where the client is that day. Coaching happens in the moment.

What are your areas of specialty?

Leadership and Change Management.

What do you go over in the first session?

How we will work together as a client and coach and review some of the pre-work that they've completed.

How long are the coaching sessions, and how often should I go?

45 minutes to an hour.

What are the benefits of having a Life Coach?

Did you ever just want someone on your side? I am really on your side. Someone to just call forth the best in you and not let you play small. That is what a real Life Coach does.

How can I tell if a Life Coach is any good?

You will know after the first session if you feel different and have a positive plan of action.

How long must I commit to working with a coach?

I suggest minimum of 3 months. Some coaches won't work with clients unless they make a 6 month commitment

Can I hire a life coach for a short-term, special project?

Of course. You can also hire different coaches for different things. I have a relationship coach that I go to with my husband and I have a coach/mentor for my own life and business.

Why would people who are already successful hire a Life Coach?

Why wouldn't someone who is successful hire a Life Coach? It isn't about being successful; it's about living a life ON purpose.

Do you offer coaching remotely, either online or over the phone, or do you only see local clients?

I offer virtual and in-person coaching services.

Please tell us how readers can get in contact with you here:

Contact Number: 866-630-6334

Email: N.Segura@MetaspireConsulting.com

Website: www.metaspireconsulting.com

CHAPTER 10

Colette D. Ellis

Please tell us about your company here:

InStep Consulting LLC is a privately-held Limited Liability Company, with headquarters in Brooklyn, New York, that helps people and organizations identify their *competent advantage*™. Since 2004, the firm has provided consulting, coaching, and training services to retained corporate and nonprofit clients throughout the United States. We seek first to understand our clients' pertinent issues and opportunities; only then do we recommend solutions that are *InStep* with their needs and priorities.

We believe that client ownership and involvement is crucial to the ultimate success of any engagement. At InStep, we foster an internal environment of openness, transparency, fun, innovation, excitement, wealth, abundance, support, education, and sharing. We make a conscious effort to retain an open mind in every client interaction. We aim to create open and safe discussion environments, and take a stand for our clients' growth, transformation and success.

What is a Life Coach, and what do you do?

A Life Coach is a partner in your journey to create the life you really want. Your coach will thoughtfully hold you accountable to make changes and take actions to fulfill your true desires. Your coach is there to guide and support you as you achieve your goals, through insightful questioning and feedback. As a Life Coach, I work with leaders who are ready to take action to turn their personal or professional setbacks into new opportunities to succeed. I help my clients to overcome their limiting beliefs and renew their enthusiasm for business, relationships and life in general.

Why would someone need a Life Coach?

You might choose to hire a Life Coach to help you develop new skills and confidence to advance in your career or take on a new business opportunity. Or you might hire a coach to help you examine how well your work-life commitments are balanced, and the impact on your personal well-being. You also might choose to hire a coach to help you adjust and rejuvenate if you have experienced a life transition; e.g., a personal loss (divorce, separation, 'empty-nesting') or a professional setback (business dissolution, downsizing).

A group or team may choose to hire a coach to help its members to develop new leadership capabilities, manage response to internal/external changes, and/or to improve interpersonal communication.

How do I select a Life Coach?

To select a Life Coach, you should first determine your goals and objectives for hiring a coach: *"What do you want to get out of working with a coach? What are you looking for in a coaching relationship?"* Then find coaches in your desired specialty area, through personal referrals or other research, and have a conversation to learn more about their skills, experience, and training. Ask the coach if s/he offers an initial discovery session for you to experience what it would be like to work with him/her. Coaching is an important relationship — you should feel a sense of connection with the coach you ultimately select to hire.

How does coaching work?

Coaching can give you a very different outlook — to transform the way you see yourself and your place in the world. It can help you focus on what matters most in your life and career or business. A coach will use dialogue to guide you through a self-discovery process to gain clarity around your personal (or professional) priorities and deepen your self-awareness so you can achieve specific goals or outcomes. A coach may use additional resources such as relevant articles, checklists, assessments or models to facilitate your thinking and better inform your choices.

How much does Life Coaching typically cost?

Working with a coach requires both a personal commitment of time and energy as well as a financial commitment. Fees charged vary by specialty and by the level of experience of the coach. You should consider both your desired benefits from coaching as well as the anticipated length of time you expect to spend being coached when making your decision to hire a coach.

What happens during a coaching session?

During your coaching engagement, you will have online or phone conversations with your coach to discuss progress towards your goals, any roadblocks you may have encountered, as well as what you are learning as a result of participating in the coaching process. Your coach will have specific questions s/he will ask to prompt you to share, and also will empower you to contribute to the focus of each conversation to ensure that you're able to discuss specific issues or concerns with which you are dealing.

In between your coaching conversations, your coach may suggest you complete targeted activities and/or take specific actions to gain greater self-awareness and insight into your situation; then your coach will provide you with feedback on your results and may suggest additional action steps for you to move forward. You will make the ultimate choice about any actions you will (or won't) take; and your coach is there to provide you with ideas, support, and accountability as needed.

What are your areas of specialty?

My areas of specialty when working with individual leaders are helping to better handle stress, manage time, and clarify personal/professional priorities. When working with groups or teams, my areas of specialty are helping to overcome conflict, and resolve interpersonal differences or breakdowns in communication.

What do you go over in the first session?

The first session is an opportunity for you and your coach to get really clear about your short and long-term goals, and the nature of the coaching relationship. It's also the chance to uncover any obstacles (internal and external) that have been holding you back from achieving those goals — often an underlying reason for you to hire a coach in the first place.

Your coach also will explore your willingness to take new actions and move out of your comfort zone to achieve your goals –

i.e., *"Is this what you REALLY want?"*

"Are you READY to make this change?"

Your coach will inspire you to visualize new possibilities and recommend next steps for you to move forward, based on his/her honest evaluation of your current situation and his/her expertise in helping others in similar situations.

How long are the coaching sessions, and how often should I go?

The length of your coaching session may vary depending on your goals for coaching and the structure of your coaching program. However, a typical session may last between 45 and 60 minutes. Again, the frequency of your coaching sessions also will vary according to your goals and program structure;

you may speak with your coach 1 - 2 times per month, and have email contact in between your conversations.

What are the benefits of having a Life Coach?

The benefits for individual leaders of working with a Life Coach include better communication and improved relationships with the important people in one's life; better health and increased energy; a renewed sense of purpose and greater enthusiasm to pursue one's goals. The benefits for a team or an organization of working with a coach include more teamwork, improved morale, more innovation, and greater clarity about direction; all of which can result in higher productivity and, ultimately, increased revenue for the organization.

How can I tell if a Life Coach is any good?

You'll know if a coach is good because s/he will listen actively to you, ask provoking yet thoughtful questions, express interest in you and your well-being, be ethical, maintain your confidentiality/privacy, and have demonstrated expertise in the area in which s/he provides coaching.

How long must I commit to working with a coach?

To increase your likelihood of achieving the goals you set at the start of coaching, it's recommended that you work with a coach for a minimum of six months. Many coaching programs, however, occur over one year or longer. You can work with your coach to determine the duration of your coaching engagement based on your goals and desired level of support and accountability.

Can I hire a life coach for a short-term, special project?

It's possible to hire a Life Coach to receive targeted support and accountability for a specific goal that you would like to achieve in a short period of time. This would likely be an accelerated coaching engagement, meaning that you might work with your coach more often (e.g., 1-2 times per week instead of 1-2 times per month) to follow a guided process that's designed to help you achieve your goal faster.

For this to be effective, you and your coach would want to be very clear about your goal and the results you're hoping to achieve as a result of the accelerated coaching process.

Such a coaching engagement might be offered at a premium since your interactions with your coach would be more frequent and customized to your individual goals (as opposed to participating in a group coaching program).

Why would people who are already successful hire a Life Coach?

Even the best athletes have coaches and personal trainers who help them to improve their skills and stay on top of their game. Similarly, people who are already successful in their careers or businesses can benefit from hiring a Life Coach to help them set even higher expectations and be able to exceed them with the right level of support and accountability to help keep them focused and motivated.

Do you offer coaching remotely, either online or over the phone, or do you only see local clients?

Yes, I offer coaching remotely via Skype and over the phone.

Please tell us how readers can get in contact with you here:

Email: info@instepconsulting.com

Web: http://www.noomii.com/users/colette-ellis

Twitter: @Coach_Colette

Facebook: https://www.facebook.com/pages/Colette-Ellis-Life-Leadership-Coach-in-Brooklyn-NY/468060433223783

Phone: 646-450-4380

Conclusion

Lives can change with the decision to pick up the phone. No matter where you are in life, a coach can help you get to whatever point you want to reach, whether it be a new career, a better relationship with your spouse, children, or faith, a more productive business, or just about anything else you can imagine.

For more information and additional resources for coaches and those seeking coaches, please visit:

www.sociaversepublishing.com/transform

www.ingramcontent.com/pod-product-compliance
Lightning Source LLC
Chambersburg PA
CBHW060952040426
42445CB00011B/1120